"Picking Up The Pieces"

by Paul King-Brown

COPYRIGHT

Paperback : ISBN 978-1-9161964-0-7

Kindle : ISBN 978-1-9161964-1-4

For more information:

www.paulkingbrown.com

ACKNOWLEDGEMENTS

"Before we start I need to thank the amazing people that love and support me. My amazing friends and family that have helped me grow, and insist that there is a better me to be explored. If I were to name them all that would be another book in itself; but you all know who you are.

However, I must thank my wife, Andrea, who loves me in such an incredible way, and is the first person to show me how to believe in myself. You are the amazing gift I treasure.

My daughter, Adina. You make me want to leave the world in a better place than I found it. You are truly inspirational, and your love truly lifts me up.

Lastly, my friend Gifford. I love our conversations, your honesty, and your sharing. Every time we speak, I take mental notes. Such is richness of your insights."

Paul King-Brown

Table of Contents

FOREWORD

No one gets married in order to divorce – well, not seriously! This is why Picking Up the Pieces by Paul King Brown is viscerally real. He got divorced. He experienced a deadly loss and for a long time was shocked, in grief, angry... But then he discovered that there was life after death. In essence, this is what this book is all about – facing the terrors of life in the darkness of divorce and discovering living again.

I am convinced that the reason why you can trust Picking Up the Pieces is because you can trust the author. It's not just words, it's Paul. It's not just facts, it's flesh and blood. It's spirit. You're meeting life behind the words. In fact, the words will dance before your very eyes and find meaningfulness in your life. So, be prepared for the journey of your life.

Paul wears his heart on his sleeve and tells it as it is. This is largely because this book has been incubating for a long time. It necessitated research by travelling inwards before travelling outwards (in interviews, listening and wrestling with hard truths). Paul had to confront himself before finding his voice. And what an amazing voice it has turned out to be – a crisp, clear, healed and being healed, soul-searching and beckoning voice. It is always on the front foot, if I may mix my metaphors.

I, therefore, invite you to read the ensuing pages not as mere facts, though factually researched they are. Neither ought you to read them as reflecting mere experience, though they are shot through by real stories. Read in between the lines, for the truth is in the tension between the researched data and the human voice. Now enjoy.

Dr Gifford Rhamie

INTRODUCTION

DIVORCE PARALYSIS

I was so excited. Christmas was going just as I had planned. The presents had been received with glee and surprise, the food was rich and the laughter was overflowing. I was truly having a merry Christmas and, seemingly, so was my entire family. I was so grateful for my life. Such was the enjoyment of the season we decided that we would all go to a party three days after the normal festivities. Unfortunately, I was unwell that evening and couldn't it to make the party, but I encouraged my wife to go along with my family anyway. I trusted her what did I have to fear? I was not a jealous person; there was no need to be. I had a great marriage, or so I thought. But five hours later on that fateful evening, I would discover that my wife was having an affair with her salsa partner.

I was hit by a huge range of colliding emotions. I was shocked, angry, confused, in intolerable pain, numb, empty, humiliated, lost, and I felt pathetic, unworthy, robbed, totally baffled and out of control, all at the same time. I was grasping at straws, grasping at anything. I was falling, falling hard and fast, such was the intensity of the emotions. How could she not need me? It simply didn't make sense.

Nearly eighteen years have passed since that day, and today, I can tell you that I am healed, at peace, content and excited by life's challenges and opportunities. But the journey to this great place has, at times, been very tough and lonely. In the beginning, I had no idea what was going on with me emotionally, so I hid what I felt with silence until the bubble had to burst. I became caught up in extremely destructive addictions and behaviors because I felt I was valueless and couldn't see anything positive to live for.

So why is letting go so difficult? This question became the bane of my existence as I struggled alone to find healing. My family and friends initially tolerated my relapses, but as the cycle of self-harm continued, it became very clear to them that I would somehow find a way to sabotage my own healing because I simply couldn't let her go. It was not that she gave me any chances of reconciliation to hang my hopes on. It would seem that I was locked in a cycle of what I now call, 'Divorce Paralysis'. I was wallowing, playing the victim. I had a string of excuses for my damaging behavior, and, consequently, I was not learning the lessons this experience was trying to teach me. I was getting in the way of my own healing. I was the block, the obstacle to my own success.

It took a while, but it soon became clear to me that I couldn't do this alone. My dark moods, the overwhelming sense of loss and a lack of reading resources made it easy for me to wallow in my divorce paralysis. But those who were concerned about me cited my social isolation and irrational behavior as clear signs that I needed to get help in coping with the trauma of dealing with infidelity. And it was within this context that I realized that I really did need to do something, or the worse fears of those around me would become a reality.

As I embarked on my journey, I started to read self-help books and looked for articles that would reassure me that this situation could be turned around. I was taking control, as I couldn't tolerate the rollercoaster of emotions that had engulfed me any more. Yet, despite my new explorations, I still felt alone and misunderstood. And so I created a close community of handpicked friends whose sole purpose was to build me up, make me accountable and aid my growth and healing. And it was while I was taking these initial steps that I encountered a Mike Murdock quote that would change my life: *"The broken become masters at mending."* It was at that moment I decided that rather than just focus on my hurt and pain, it was incumbent on me to reach out to others and assist, to play a part where possible in the healing of others who had suffered the same fate.

This course consists of an accumulation of experiences and insights from my perspective of being a victim of infidelity; but more importantly, there are also the understandings that I have gained from my role as a Pastor. I have listened to and counselled many who have shed countless tears and become caught up in intense pain and frustration by focusing on the hurt and not taking positive action steps. But I have also had the pleasure to witness the transformation of those who have committed themselves to the healing journey and have watched with excitement as they arrived at a wonderful place of breakthrough, healing and ultimate joy.

The journey begins with the stone-cold reality of divorce paralysis. This opening introduction hurts because it eloquently brings you face to face with your trauma. This is necessary before you can come to grips with the important steps to recovery. For that's how the chapters are coined: '**steps**'. Seven steps. Seven steps, that are not linear in logic, but overlap organically and unpredictably, each ending with a practical strategy to take the reader forward. That's because they're human steps. *Step 1* seeks to process you through your trauma: 'Coping with Trauma'. Trauma, that finds expression through different kinds of emotional wounds and scars. This begins to make sense in *Step 2,* 'Rebuilding your Confidence'. Here, Paul takes us through the stages of denial, anger, bargaining, depression and acceptance as we face loneliness in learning to listen to our own heartbeat.

This is why *step 3* must follow: 'Getting Support'. There are different kinds of support – personal and professional. Indeed, the burden begins to lift when you discover that you're not alone. Yet, most of your healing comes through reckoning with *step 4*: 'Forgiveness and Letting Go of Bitterness'. You will find the rhythm and cadence of this chapter consoling. No, there's no quick fix formula. Forgiveness is like a faithful well that is revisited. Its depth forever surprises you with fresh healing. Only when you revisit it does *step 5* makes sense: 'Creating a New Life'. It is filled with nuggets such as, 'do more of what makes you happy', 'be careful how you talk to yourself', 'act as if', 'pass it on', and 'surround yourself with the right people'.

Step 6 is particularly challenging if you have children. But read it you must. Then again, *step 7* is the ultimate: 'Walking into your Healing'. You see your life in motion, but in colour. Its appeal is its realism. Myths are punctured, where you are let down gently. But hope is restored as you visualize your coming into being as wellness and growth.

In this book you will go from feeling heartbroken, angry and disoriented to feeling back in control, restored and empowered as you experience a renewed sense of purpose, value, acceptance and peace. In order for the process to work, it is essential that you intentionally set goals for yourself along the way, that you are fully committed to creating new healthy habits that will rebuild your confidence and self-esteem, that you understand that the process will require you to access a support network or community, realizing that you cannot do this alone, and lastly, that you see this course as a foundational platform from which you will leap to meet the new challenges and opportunities that will come your way. Step One of the process is simply making and acting on the statement, "I want to be healed."

SO LET'S BEGIN!!!!

STEP 1

COPING WITH THE TRAUMA

"There are wounds that never show on the body that are deeper and more hurtful than anything that bleeds."-Laurell K. Hamilton

I don`t exactly remember all the details, but my parents didn't attend a parents' evening or receive a school report for me from the ages of 12 to 14. From my recollection, I did receive the reports, but I was so scared of my father's reaction that I threw them away. That was because, in our house, we were only allowed to get As. Any grades that were lower spelt disaster for you. I knew that I had some As, but my reports were also littered with other letters of the alphabet that were considered unacceptable. As you can probably guess, a teacher cottoned on to my three-year-long process of hiding and deceit and, rather than giving me the report, delivered it directly to my father, asking him how it compared to the previous reports. I will always remember that day because it was on that fateful Thursday I was confronted with my actions and had to deal with the consequences that ensued. I remember thinking that three years of discipline in one day was too much to bear. But I also realised that I did not have to deal with the burden and the guilt of hiding, that I could deal with the failures as well as the successes of my education. I remember after the pain subsided that I wished I had dealt with this head-on from the beginning.

Dealing with the trauma and devastation of divorce is different for all of us. We react and respond in so many varied ways, and there is no manual on how to react in these situations. I remember a client telling me of the devastation of his divorce. He told me that, as he was packing and leaving the family home, none of his three children told him that they would miss him. None of them tried to persuade him to stay. As he recounted this painful scene to me, I could sense that a deep wound still resided within him, as their lack of compassion towards him had caused him to question their love for him. Years later, he said that he had spoken to his eldest son about that moment and the reaction, or non-reaction, he had from his children. He said that the response of his eldest to him revealing this wound was astonishing. His son said, "Dad, I was in shock too. I didn't know how to behave. In fact, from the day you left, part of me has always been numb." As my client came to the end of the sentence, tears were dripping down both cheeks.

In this chapter, I want to talk to you about how to cope emotionally with the break-up of your marriage. Let me first say that I have discovered through experience and research that when someone wants to leave and has no desire to continue the marriage, you cannot do anything to make them stay. Not even double backflips with a 2.3 degree of difficulty—but they won't stay. So, whenever someone is determined to leave you, you have to let him or her go. But most importantly, the message I want to give you but that you will not want to hear: "IT IS NOT YOUR FAULT."

You will play the video over and over again in your head. You will say to yourself, "If only I had done this, it would all be so different. This would never have happened." But I'm here to tell you that whatever you could have done would have made no difference to someone who was hell-bent on taking a course of action that gave them excitement but would ultimately destroy your life. You need to really understand: "IT IS NOT YOUR FAULT."

This feeling of helplessness, this loss of control, this sense of futility is very real and needs to be confronted so that you can heal and become a newer, revived you. Overworking, being over-busy and living in a state of constant denial are very unhealthy habits that can end up being a stumbling block to your healing. I understand that psychology 101 tells us that human beings love pleasure and will do anything to resist pain. But in this process, it is paramount that the pain that emanates from divorce is confronted and dealt with. Avoidance, though understandable and at times easier, is detrimental to your healing and growth. But let me emphasise that the sadness you feel is not your final destination, as you have the strength, determination and resolve within you to get all you desire for yourself.

And so here I'm going to give you a few tools that will help you cope with the trauma of divorce:

Firstly, you will experience an array of painful emotions, and they will come in waves. Some will overwhelm you, and some you will be able to deal with. But the key is to feel every emotion. Be aware of the anxiety, the stress and the fear. It will be penetrating, but accept that you will have varying degrees and intensities of different feelings. Some you will have felt before, and some will be new and will threaten your being to its core. Coping with these feelings head-on is necessary; if you don't deal with them and instead try and bury them, you need to know that they will not disappear but will re-emerge at an inopportune time in your life. So I'm asking you to accept the challenge and start the process of dealing with the feelings of loss, disappointment, hurt and betrayal that you feel right now.

Secondly, go and see a qualified counsellor. The duration of using a counsellor is very much dependent on your own personal needs, but, from experience and listening to many of my clients, I can tell you that discussing coping mechanisms with a qualified counsellor is a foundational building block on your road to healing and restoration. This is because understanding the coping mechanisms that will work for you is a crucial and decisive element in your healing. Think of it as that flicker of light that will illuminate the darkest places in your journey.

Thirdly, make time for you. Focus on you. Soothe you. Cuddle you. Be nicer to you.

Earlier in this book, we spoke about stopping. Taking the time to be aware of where you are, how you feel, and taking steps to make yourself feel better. Divorce, by its nature, brings intense pain, resentment and bitterness. You will also be over-sensitive and paranoid at times. All of this is natural, since now you are reacting to the notion that you are where you are as a consequence of you not paying attention to your partner within the marriage. You think that this lack of attention is the cause of the break-up. But this isn't entirely true. True, your negative feelings are very real and pronounced, but it is an oversimplification to place what has happened at the door of your own inattention'.

So taking time to reflect and form new positive habits allows the calming balm of peace and healing to re-energise you.

In this time of reforming your life, you are presented with a unique opportunity to refocus your identity, to remodel and sharpen who you are. You can now do all the things you have always wanted to do but were too busy. Now is a great time to pamper yourself. Do a yoga class or go to the gym. Take dance classes or dust the bike off and ride like the wind with your friends through a nature park. Listen to your favourite music, savour a hot bath. Whatever you dream up, do that. Savour the refreshing positive feelings that being in that environment brings, as it's important that you pay attention to what you need emotionally.

Lastly, it is critical that you avoid destructive habits. As tempting as it is to relieve feelings of pain and loneliness through the excessive use of alcohol, drugs or food, these kinds of instant gratification create a cycle of abuse that can have catastrophic effects on your emotional well-being and your subsequent healing. You should also avoid gambling and promiscuity. Avoid acting out on angry impulses. Although initially, these behaviours may be pleasurable, the mid- and long-term negative effects have an adverse impact on your journey of healing.

One last thing that I have discovered will have a lasting effect on your ability to cope with the effects of divorce is writing a journal. You don't have to stick to a daily regimented schedule, but writing down how you are currently feeling gives you a fantastic outlet and mode of expression. Plus, it will give you a guide against which you can measure how much you have grown as you overcome the issues that arise from divorce.

COPING WITH TRAUMA STRATEGY:

1. Get a Divorce Coach and qualified counsellor
2. Be careful how you speak to yourself. It`s important to focus on positive self-talk.
3. Remodel your life. Try new things.
4. Avoid destructive behaviour and habits.

STEP 2

REBUILDING CONFIDENCE AND SELF-ESTEEM

"It's not the mountain we conquer but ourselves."

Sir Edmund Hilary

One day, I was invited to the funeral of a close friend's relative. I didn't know the person who had died very well, but we would occasionally meet at family gatherings. Obviously, for my friend, the bereavement cut deep, and I was glad that I was able to be of support to someone I cared about. Also, his pain became a momentary distraction from my own. Looking back, it gave me the first glimpse into how focusing on someone else's needs can be a soothing balm for your own hurt.

When the day of the funeral arrived, I made myself available to the family to assist with any duties that would help make the process more bearable for them. As the beautiful funeral service commenced, I didn't know what was happening, but a deep sense of loss gripped me. I became overwhelmed by emotion as I sat there, and I started to cry. Initially, it was a light whimper, but soon I was crying like I had never cried before. Throughout it all, part of me was thinking, "Why am I crying so much? I didn't even know this person that well." Yet the grief I was expressing was real and authentic.

A little time later, I once again questioned myself and reflected on why my emotions had gotten the better of me. And soon it became clear to me what was going on. I had suppressed my anger, grief and deep sense of loss for a long time. I had been to my ex's father-in-law's funeral previously and had shown no emotion that day. He was truly a great man, someone that I had loved, but on that day, nothing. It was all bottled up. But one day, somehow it all had to come out.

Science has shown us that suppressing our emotions does not bode well for our emotional health. In fact, the consequences of this suppression can manifest themselves in depression, stress, mood swings, unexplained sadness, low self-esteem and even mild depression. Such is the extent that what is hidden needs to be expressed that it is reported that suppressed emotions will find manifest themselves even in your dreams.

Scientists found in a 1987 study that the more you try to suppress an emotion or thought, the higher the likelihood of it exhibiting itself. Such is the vicious cycle of this suppression—it would seem that the more you try, the more trouble and negative feelings you are creating for yourself. Even though heaping more pain onto your existence was not your intention, that is exactly what you are doing to yourself by behaving in this way.

When you feel a need to suppress your emotions, the key is to learn new and healthier strategies to regulate them instead. One of the first such strategies is recognizing what you are doing and where you are emotionally. I like to call this, "Being real with yourself."

Now here is some 'Breaking News' I want you to take on board: you are grieving. Yes, you heard me correctly, I said "grieving." The grieving process is typically categorized into five stages: Denial, Anger, Bargaining, Depression Acceptance. And it is within this grieving process that your emotions are being expressed but are also becoming very distorted. Hence, it is important not only to be present and actively and intentionally engage with your own healing but to be aware of your location within this emotional process, as the pain will play tricks with you and at times send you the wrong signals. You need to accept that your decision-making, thinking and clarity will be somewhat inaccurate and impaired as you go through this post break-up journey.

Secondly, and I do need you to take this on board, time alone does not heal. Intentional behavior, a commitment to the process, making a plan and accessing great support mechanisms are all central to your healing. Time alone, as we know from the penal system, leaves people bitter and seeking revenge. Your healing will require you to be present in the place where you really are, and if that is pain, pain is where you are. To deceive yourself, as I did, can stall or even reverse the progress you are making. However, repeated, constantly practiced steps in the direction of an emotionally healthier you will be key to your healing and success.

At this point, it would be easy to gloss over some of the terms mentioned within this chapter, but I want to return to the significance of you knowing where you are in the context of the grieving process. Having this awareness and recognition of your environment will assist you to see the full picture of how you are progressing and better gauge your recovery.

1. DENIAL:

I had a diary. In this diary were the details of my life. Not just small details, but every detail. And for the first two years of my break-up and subsequent divorce, I used that diary to CREATE A LIFE I WAS NOT LIVING, a fake life, if you will. Its main focus was weekends, when I supposedly went to endless parties and took numerous short weekend breaks with my imaginary friends. Writing this diary enabled me to lie to those around me, as I couldn't tell anyone the truth—that my wife had had an affair and left me. And so, to my work colleagues, my real life was the life in the diary, but in reality, it was total fiction, as I lived life in a dark abyss of pain, not seeing a way out. I was in denial.

Denial is the first stage of grieving, coming to your aid when the full ramifications of your loss are too much to handle all at once. In this initial stage, denial protects you from the full emotional hurt that you are experiencing.

2. ANGER:

Even though denial is considered the first stage in the grieving process, pain and anger are a close second. This is because the trauma felt brings with it a total loss of control. It feels as though you have been in a massive crash and someone else is at the wheel of your life, with you simply being the passenger. The impact is intense as you try to understand how someone you loved and cared for could consider inflicting the excruciating, life-altering pain that a break-up like this brings.

Due to the massive injustice of this situation, you may feel at this stage that you want to lash out and hit back in a rush of anger that is deeply correlated to the pain of your break-up experience. Stalking your ex or even having fantasies of violence can never be endorsed, but due to the injustices of it all, these extremes exist. Yet, the direct and focused expression of this anger can be used as a platform for our future healing and fulfilment. Hence, our anger in reflection isn't a wasted commodity but, in time, is a conduit to a better place.

3. BARGAINING:

In this stage, you will find yourself doing anything, and I mean anything, to get back to the place where you thought that you were in control and where you were not in so much pain. The pain drives you to do anything that could make it all go away. This stage is difficult, but your need to be needed is in direct conflict with the holistic healing that can be yours. I would be told that I deserved better, but I didn't want better: I wanted her. As ridiculous as that sounds now, then, it was a key principle of my existence. I was willing to trade everything for just a morsel of her attention, such was my need to dismiss the pain. But the advice I was given was correct: there are richer relationships, opportunities and experiences that will come your way soon. This is in no way the end of the road for you. The pain can deceive you into believing in negative outcomes for your life. By now, you are learning how to figure out where you are and then resist. It will take time, but you will get stronger.

4. DEPRESSION:

Not being able to save my marriage brought a feeling of total helplessness coupled with a total and utter loss of self. I was on a life-support system, numb, and the

depression led to severe voluntary isolation. I wanted to be left alone, as I was drowning in hopelessness. I was useless, unworthy of a relationship and I had a certificate to prove it. This gave me an excuse to poison my body with my addictions, as I felt that no one cared, including myself. I just wanted to be left alone in this abyss. In depression, you see no light at the end of the tunnel, and this is an unhealthy place to be. But be alert to the fact that you are just passing through this stage—you don't live here.

5. ACCEPTANCE:

For me, it was at this stage that I grew up. It was at this stage I became most reflective and analytical, rather than over-emotional, reactive and out of control. With the onset and growth of acceptance, I began to realize that though I didn't instigate the breakdown of my marriage or destroy it, I still played a part in its failure. It was at this stage that I stopped the pity party and began to look at myself to explore which traits and behaviors I displayed that could have provoked my ex into leaving me. In acceptance, I could see the green shoots of a new sustainable me. This was an enriching and empowering place to be, as in the acceptance stage, I was able to see that I had grown and that a better me was emerging from the fog of my grief.

Now that I have explained the grief process and you have discovered your place in it, I need you to understand that the stages do not necessarily advance in a straight line, where the next stage starts when the last one finishes. You may discern that they overlap, go back on themselves and repeat. And there is no telling how long each stage will last. But the great thing about being orientated and knowing where you are, is that you will note that you are still standing and you have not faded away with the pain. In time you will see that you are made of more than you have ever known.

REBUILDING CONFIDENCE STRATEGY:

1. Acknowledge where you are emotionally.
2. Stop blaming yourself
3. Look your best
4. Make the most of every new day

STEP 3

GETTING SUPPORT

"I'll wait for you, and if I fall behind, wait for me."

Bruce Springsteen

To win the World Triathlon title in 2016, Johnny Brownlee needed to finish first in the final race of the season and his Spanish competitor needed to finish fourth. It would seem that all was going to plan, but around 100 km before the finishing line, Johnny noticed that his brother, Alastair, who was also in the race, had begun to weave from side to side, totally disoriented by the fatigue brought on by this arduous race. Rather than keep on running, Johnny turned back mid-race to carry his brother over the finishing line. Johnny lost the race, but the race will always be remembered for something more valiant than running 26 miles, swimming 60 km and cycling 55 miles. This race will forever live in the annals of sporting history because of the unconditional support one brother gave to another.

As I was reading the accounts of the race, it reminded me of the first time I saw a song sung by Bruce Springsteen and the E Street Band. The song's lyrics were haunting as every member sang the same lyrics and echoed the same theme, "I'll wait for you, and if I fall behind, wait for me." There is something amazing about a community of people, friends who decide that they are there for you through thick and thin. And these people not only say it; their actions demonstrate their support for you.

The journey of divorce lends itself initially to denial and shock and hence, isolation. The shock of it all makes you retreat, because recovering from this blow is very personal and, for a lot of people, very private. The self-loathing, shame and humiliation that comes with the discovery of a betrayal is deeply debilitating and brings intense pain. When faced with this, it is almost natural that you would recoil to a secluded place where you can be alone to tend to your wounds.

You will remember from the last chapter what I told you about my post-breakup diary—the diary where I detailed a whole fake life of friends, parties and a happy life. The diary provided me with lies to tell those around me when I couldn't cope with the shame, the stench of negative emotions and the stigma of being less. And so I fed my work colleagues the life recorded in the diary while hiding in my world of pain, totally withdrawn, and not seeing a way out. My head was saying, "Shhhhhhhhhhhh", but my heart needed some urgent help.

Creating a support structure or support group is an essential part of your healing, as the desire to withdraw is detrimental to your ultimate recovery.

There will be legal issues, financial issues, parenting issues and emotional, physical and well-being issues that may feel too overwhelming to deal with. There will be decisions that need your urgent attention and clarity of mind, even though you are suffering from the consequences of divorce.

This weight, let's call it a burden, is best shouldered by creating a structure of support that enables you to come to the best decisions due to being surrounded by those who have your best interests at heart. This is because it is difficult to make good decisions alone, especially from a place of pain and uncertainty.

I would suggest that your support group(s) should consist of a legal adviser, financial advisor, counsellor, exercise trainer and divorce coach. Having these experts working on your behalf for the improvement of your cause is foundational to your healing. Support groups are a strong anchor to objectivity in this turbulent time.

One of the things you will recognise is that you will be repeating the story of your divorce constantly. It will be as though this is the only thing you have to talk about. This is mainly because you are replaying this situation over and over again internally, trying to figure out how you got here. You are working through a state of shock because you didn't see it coming. However, you will also discover that some friends will get bored with this. They will treat you as though you have a contagious disease called

'Divorce'. Hence, it is important that your support group consists of mature and supportive friends who are truly empathetic about your pain and are willing to listen and support you, come what may. Some of your friends will not have all the answers, but their being there for you is a vital element to your healing. You will discover on this journey that the quality of your empathic and compassionate friends can determine the tempo of your healing as your process the pain.

Before we finish this step, I just want to tell you why each support team member is valuable and their function in your healing process:

Legal Advisor: Divorce brings up complex legal issues that will often be new to you, and many obstacles may arise that need expert opinions and guidance.

Financial Advisor: Having taken legal advice, it will now be time to look at your assets and how these may need to be re-distributed. Issues such as selling the family home or running two homes need an expert capable of precision and clarity, as getting the resolution of these issues wrong could be very expensive.

Counsellor: A qualified counsellor is critical, as you will need to be taught coping mechanisms that will help with the rollercoaster of negative emotions that surround the devastation of divorce. A counsellor is an important part of your healing.

Exercise Trainer: It will be very easy to neglect your physical health. Isolation, low self-esteem, a lack of pride and shame are all emotions that will lead you to a place of bad eating, bad hygiene and general un-healthiness. A trainer will give you a schedule and a regular routine. They will even accompany you whenever you work out if that is what it takes for you to remain healthy through this ordeal.

Divorce Coach: A good divorce coach is indispensable to this process, as the experts mentioned above all charge by the hour, but divorce coaches are there for your emotional health at all times. They are there for you when you are overwhelmed by all the decisions that you have to make. As you reflect on the past and project to the future, a good divorce coach reassures you and makes you aware that, within the chaos, you are in control. Good divorce coaches are empowering, compassionate, inspiring and very aware of the process of healing that is necessary for a renewed and revived you.

Let me just add that you may have other needs that require an additional expert or someone empathic to specific needs. That's ok! The essence of this chapter is that you don't have to try to do life alone. You will attempt to do so, but your healing will be better served by allowing good people into your life who are more than willing to help you if you let them.

A very wise man once said, "A person standing alone can be attacked and defeated, but two can stand back-to-back and conquer. Three are even better together and are not easily broken."(Ecclesiastes 4:12)

SUPPORT STRATEGY:

1.Write a journal, but don't fall into isolation

2.Connect to a supportive community

3.Get a Divorce Coach and a counsellor

4.Do not do life alone

STEP 4

FORGIVENESS AND LETTING GO OF BITTERNESS

"The weak can never forgive. Forgiveness is the attribute of the strong."-Mahatma Gandhi

There are many variations to this story, so for this chapter's purposes, we will simply describe this tale as the 'Monkey Trap'. The story is told that in order to catch a monkey, you hollow out a coconut and place a banana inside the shell. When the monkey grabs the banana, its hand is trapped inside, and the only way to escape this trap is for the monkey to let go of the banana. But such is the monkey's fixation on getting the banana, the monkey cannot figure out that to be free and not be in the trap, it needs to let go.

When I first heard this analogy, I knew that it was referring to me. Because forgiving has to be the hardest single thing I have had to deal with and master. I initially behaved like an entitled narcissist, as I believed a different set of rules applied to me. My wife had had an affair, and the attachment was so deep for me that I found it enormously hard to sever myself from the marriage emotionally and move on. The anguish of being the rejected partner was devastating. Some people experience unending grief, overwhelming pessimism and a deepening fear that love might never happen for them again. That was me. The irony was that, as I was quietly suffering, I spent many hours professionally in counselling sessions with deeply saddened, abandoned partners who couldn't get past their losses. As I listened to their stories and their confusion over why they couldn't seem to make love last, I was thinking, "Just let go of the banana." But, as we all know, it's easier said than done.

When you are involved in conversations about forgiveness and you are not the hurt party, you will often hear the phrases, "All I need from them is to say they're sorry," or "All I need is an apology." But, as you are aware, being involved in an infidelity whirlwind demands far more than the platitudes you once thought were sufficient for moving on. Such is the range of irrational emotions that all logic and reasonableness would seem to get thrown out of the window. The anger, the disbelief, the envy and the jealousy make for an explosive cocktail of emotions. Such is the feeling of being disorientated by infidelity that you begin to get excited by the small emotional crumbs that are sporadically thrown your way, such is the hurt's clamour for validation and renewed acceptance.

I remember when, six months after the separation from my ex, she called me to arrange a meeting. I was so excited, as every communiqué from me was normally met with a wall of silence, but this time she seemed more open. For two days, the pain of the past seemed to disappear in my excitement about the idea of our meeting. I guess I can only put my mood down to the fact that I had watched too many romantic comedies with happy endings because she gave me no indication that reconciliation was on the cards. When the day arrived, we met, and at the end of our meeting, she casually informed me that her lover had dumped her. At this moment, I was convinced that reconciliation was possible, that all could be forgiven and that we could just reset our relationship immediately. But as she spoke, her words pierced my heart, and new hurt bloomed within me as she relayed to me her pain, suffering and longing to be reunited with him. Imagine the one you love telling you how deeply they love someone else, and at the same time, people are telling you to forgive. Unsurprisingly, anger and bitterness surged up within me that dwarfed the lifting of my mood over the preceding few days. Forgiveness was the last thing on my mind.

On reflection, I have to be honest and tell you that, as the hurt party, I played the victim. Not having the tools, wisdom and resources to heal, I wallowed in my pain and complained constantly to my friends and family. Consequently, I had many people feeling sorry for me. But that unforgiving mind set was not good for me. I was going nowhere; I started to get sick of hearing myself whinge, and at a certain point, I knew I had to take responsibility for the way I was living life. And so, I started to research 'forgiveness.'

The scenario that challenged me was the work of Simon Wiesenthal, a holocaust survivor and a man who dedicated his life to finding Nazi war criminals who had escaped justice. In his book, The Sunflower, he told of how he would be confronted with numerous opportunities to forgive, but such was the hurt caused and the depth of the atrocities that he felt that it was not his place to forgive. Though his stance could not be questioned, his refusal to forgive obviously troubled him, as in the second edition of his book he solicited the opinions of many famous people, asking them whether his being unforgiving was indeed correct. As I read the accounts, it became clear to me that not forgiving is a poison, a bitterness, if you will, that resides in the one who refuses to forgive. It was at this stage that I came to the conclusion that by forgiving, I would be aiding my own healing. Lewis Smedes says, "To forgive is to set a prisoner free and discover that the prisoner was you."

Having discovered this new pathway, I declared to myself that something within me had to change; that my blame game had to stop and that I had to take ownership of how I was going to address those who had hurt me. I knew that I couldn't remain in this dead-end cycle of hurt and revenge; it was time to let go of the banana.

As I forged ahead on my newfound quest, I tried to start the day with a more positive and productive attitude rather than letting my emotional pain dictate my life. The pain was there, but I now started to take intentional steps to not letting bitterness and anger determine how I was living. I started the day by simply being grateful for life, for little things like the sun or the rain, for my daughter. I began by just introducing gratefulness into my existence, and even though the pain wanted me to return to my ungratefulness and complaints, I fought it, every day.

Another thing I did was to deepen my research into what forgiveness really was. I had tried to forget what had been done to me, but that hadn't worked. So I challenged myself to seek out how other hurt people expressed and embraced forgiveness. It was through this that I discovered a few quotes that motivated me to dig deeper:

"I forgive you. I will never use it against you in the future. I will never speak of it again to you or anyone else." —Mark Gungor

"You will know that forgiveness has begun when you recall those who hurt you and feel the power to wish them well."—Lewis B. Smedes

"It takes one person to forgive, it takes two people to be reunited." —Lewis B. Smedes

"Without forgiveness, there's no future." —Desmond Tutu

When I initially read these quotes, I knew that I could never truly forgive. How could I ever come to the place where I would want to wish my ex's lover well? I had used my hurt as leverage and collateral for so long that to be freed from it would have left me empty. As I was confronted with this new notion of forgiveness, I reflected on the night I discovered my ex's infidelity, and, in desperation, I had called her lover and begged him not to take my family away from me. I had humiliated myself in front of him, and now I was reading a quote that suggested that my healing was dependent on me sending good thoughts his way. This was difficult to digest, process and then execute, but as I wanted to be free, I vowed that the pain was no longer going to determine my future. It was within this mindset that I encountered the South African Truth and Reconciliation Commission.

In 1984, Bishop Desmond Tutu and President F.W. DeKlerk won the Nobel Prize for their mission to add the spiritual discipline of forgiveness to a situation that would normally require a war crimes tribunal. Tutu came up with the idea that in order for South Africa to heal from the wounds of Apartheid, transparency and reconciliation needed to be forged between those who had caused the pain and the victims of their actions. Hence, this process led to both sides confronting each other with the ultimate goal being that the future South Africa would be a unified entity once everyone involved had both confessed and understood the gravity of the distress caused. This process was very painful as the truths of the crimes were revealed, but the leaders were looking for a new united South Africa to emerge from the forgiveness that permeated this process. As I read the accounts, I was very aware that the journey of forgiveness would be fruitful but that it would not be easy. A whole range of negative emotions would rear their ugly heads, but this was a necessary stage in my quest to emotional freedom from the hurt.

Jo Berry went through a similar process as she decided that she wanted to meet the IRA bomber that had killed her father, Sir Anthony Berry, in the Brighton hotel bombings in 1984:

"I chose to give up blame and revenge, instead taking responsibility for my pain and feelings, transforming them into passion for peace. The journey of healing began with my intention and I trusted that life would then bring me the opportunities to heal and grow."

When you listen to Jo speak, you become very aware of her pain, but you are also struck by the realization that within this horrendous experience there is empathy, compassion and a desire for peace, not revenge. She recalls that this was mindset forged by an incidental meeting at a taxi rank with a stranger whose brother had been killed by British soldiers. She remarked that they both felt the same pain but from different sides, and this irony was not lost on her.

Many years later, my ex-wife told me that her decision had devastated her, that she didn't know she was capable of such an indiscretion and the decisions that followed. She told me how her decision to never return to me was not based on love but on the fact that she never wanted to inflict that kind of hurt on another human being again. As I listened, I became acutely aware that she was in pain too. Admittedly, I didn't sympathize with or want to hear about her pain, as she had put this rollercoaster in motion. But as she spoke, my visions of her having a wonderful time as I suffered were somewhat dispelled. My pain and brokenness had made me entirely self-centered, and it was only when I started to embrace the idea of forgiveness that empathy and compassion for those outside of myself began to grow. I began to notice that I was becoming more sensitive to the needs of others. Before, I had no idea how to be genuinely sympathetic to others. Practicing forgiveness had begun to change my world.

FORGIVENESS STRATEGY:

1. Acknowledge the hurt. Confront the pain.
2. Recognise that hurting is part of the process.
3. Forgive yourself. Release the need to be in control.
4. Plant good seeds of kindness, regardless of the pain.
5. Your freedom and peace are on the other side of forgiveness. Keep going.
6. In doing this, you are creating a safe place for your heart to be loved again. A place of joy and giving, and a place where you can love yourself again too.

STEP 5

CREATING A NEW LIFE

"There will come a time when you believe everything is finished; that will be the beginning."-Louis L`Armour

I used to visit Norway years ago. It is such a beautiful country with great people. Yet, despite my great memories of the Norwegians, one very valuable lesson I learned was to be very careful when a Norwegian invites you to the beach or asks you to go for a walk.

I remember the first time I was asked to go to the beach, only to get there and watch as my friends proceeded to remove what I can only describe as heavy machinery from the boot of their car. I realized then that we were not going to swim, relax, get a tan and eat ice cream. We were going to climb up a sheer rock face by the beach then abseil down. This was no place for just a pair of speedos.

Of course, it took me a few invites to realise that the Norwegians loved the outdoors and nature and the challenges that extreme conditions bring. On one of these occasions, I was invited to go for a walk near my friend's summerhouse. What he should have said was that we were going to climb a mountain, because that is exactly what we did. I'll be upfront about it: I didn't want to climb this mountain or any other mountain. I love the Netherlands; it's flat. But here I was, climbing a mountain.

It was tough, and I decided almost before we really began that I would not and could not make it to the top. There were about twelve of us walking at different paces, and the further we went, the more disconnected I became from the main group. I didn't mind, because as everyone was moving forward, I was planning on heading back. Just as I had become comfortable with my decision to turn back, one of my friends, Evan, came back to get me. Without addressing my lack of confidence and slow pace, he told me that when his father first took him up these mountains, he hated this walk. (Yes, I knew the feeling.) But his father used to tell him stories; lots of stories, so many stories that when his father stopped telling him stories, he discovered that he had reached the top of the mountains. "What type of stories did he tell you?" I asked. He replied that the stories were always about people who conquered their fears and met challenges not by being the strongest or the bravest but by simply refusing to give up.

When Evan's stories stopped, we had reached the top. It was an amazing view. I had done it. I raised my hands like that scene from 'Rocky'. Overcoming this challenge was exhilarating and gave me an overwhelming feeling of accomplishment. My confidence was sky-high. I had done it, and I couldn't wait to climb another mountain.

"Confidence is built on achieving." Firstly, as you start to rebuild and enhance your confidence during the ordeal of your break-up and divorce, it is imperative that you set goals and endeavour to achieve them. They don't have to be relationship goals; any goal, any new achievement is good, as the feeling of triumph it will give you will make you feel great about yourself. Secondly, and as important, is that your success sends the message to your self-esteem that you are a person of value and significance. You can do stuff!

I don't know if you've ever been on a diet, but during my dieting days I noticed something quite incredible: success with my dieting gave rise to a sense of discipline and achievement in other areas of my life. Because I was disciplined in one area of my life, it was seemingly easier to deal with other issues and be as disciplined elsewhere. Rebuilding your confidence and self-esteem is an essential part of your healing and needs your full commitment and participation. Here, I want to give you five principles that will help you rediscover how amazing you are:

1. DO MORE OF WHAT MAKES YOU HAPPY

I have spoken to many clients who have told me that part of the bitterness and hurt they are suffering from the break-up comes from the fact that they gave everything to the relationship and never focused on their own needs. Though where you are may be undeserved, you are now presented with a unique opportunity to focus solely on you, an opportunity to excel, thrive and succeed for you. Many have spoken about running for a charity, learning how to play the piano, or giving more of their time to their community projects. Whatever it is that makes you happy, do it. Whatever stirs your passions and leaves you energised, do it! The repetition, over and over again, of achievements within something you enjoy will reinforce the fact that you are a person of substance, worth, a person who accomplishes whatever you choose to do, hence creating a self you will admire.

2. BE CAREFUL HOW YOU TALK TO YOURSELF

I'm sure you've heard people say that they are their own worst critic. I must tell you that this isn't just a cliché but also a real, living truth. Many people don't speak to themselves very nicely and often repeat and amplify the negative words of others. We only need to look at our childhoods and reflect on how the negative words of others have become burdens that we have carried around with us for years.

And so, it is essential that you begin to speak uplifting words of affirmation to yourself. No longer will you be a critic; from this day onwards, you will be an encourager, your own number one fan. Bad self-talk is harmful and is damaging to your healing. I remember I used to tell a joke that my divorce certificate was a paper confirmation that I was a failure. I joked about this all the time until someone told me that I had to stop talking to myself in that way. I didn't think of it as self-harm at the time, but in the period of my life when I was making such 'jokes', all attempts at a healthy relationship failed abysmally. I was living out the negative thoughts I had about myself.

Yet I must confess that despite every effort I initially made during my healing journey to eradicate negative self-talk, I didn't do it very well. Years of this self-debilitating habit had taken its toll. But I'm glad to announce to you that I found a way to speak to myself in more positive and glowing terms. I now focus on the positive words. I'm no longer concerned about the negative. Now my sole focus is amplifying the words of empowerment and inspiration to such an extent that the amplification drowns out the negative. This is how I climbed the mountain we mentioned earlier. The positive stories silenced and dispelled my negative thoughts of failure. I began to hear, "You can do it" and "There is no quit in me." Every step became easier as the positivity washed over me. I believe that this feeling can be yours, too.

3. ACT AS IF

Some call it "Fake it 'til you make it." I have called this step "Act as if." We both know that in some regard you are already doing this. Divorce is a label and identity that is not you. You're not a stigma. It drags you down; it tells you that you are unworthy. Yet you have to function as a colleague, a sibling, a parent, a person with responsibilities. I'm asking that you do everything in your power (and I know you might not have a lot of that) to keep up your standards of health, hygiene and presentation. Reimagine yourself. Dress for success, even if you don't feel like it. Eventually, your interior will catch up with your exterior. Avoid the destructive habits of isolation and focus on being the best you possibly can.

4. PASS IT ON

One of the most profound statements I have ever read was that "The broken are masters at mending." I didn't truly grasp the depth of that statement until I encountered the workings of Alcoholics Anonymous. I met people who were vulnerable, lost and hurting but yet concerned enough about others in pain to be part of a process that helps others on their road to healing within the AA program. I saw the wonderful power of community, genuine compassion and accountability working at its best. Giving of themselves not only contributed to the healing of others but also aided their own. There is a very old song that says, "Give, and it will come back to you." There is something uniquely powerful in seeing hurt people give to others who are also in pain. John Maxwell, in his book, Winning with People, echoes the power of these principles by talking about the power of what he calls, 'Elevator People'. His contention is that you have the power to bring people down or lift people up. He speaks enthusiastically about the positive power of being surrounded by people whose motivation is to see a better you. This indeed is a rich cycle of healing to be involved with.

5. SURROUND YOURSELF WITH THE RIGHT PEOPLE

If you've had any discussions with parents with teenagers, you will have observed that one of the major concerns as they bring their children up is the type of friends they choose to hang around with. Engaged parents are acutely aware that the health and well-being of their child are as seriously impacted by their choice of friends as they are by the morals and ethics instilled at home. A bad set of friends brings with it worries and concerns that are not just about the immediate but the long term. Hence, being surrounded by the right people has an enriching and empowering effect that brings out the best in all of us. On your journey, be prepared to make new friends, as some of the old friends, though well-meaning, will not understand the transitions that are going on in your life. They may perceive going back as a good thing, but you will realise more and more that it is critical that you surround yourself with people who are willing to encourage you all the way in your new journey until you get to the top of your mountain.

CREATING A NEW LIFE STRATEGY:

1. Do whatever stirs your passions and leaves you energised.
2. Speak to yourself in more positive and glowing terms.
3. "Act as if" life is amazing, and, eventually, it will be.
4. Focus on the needs of others and give yourself to other people.
5. Surround yourself with good people.

STEP 6

CO-PARENTING

"The best security blanket a child can have is parents who respect each other."-Jane Blaustone

In conducting surveys with clients who had been divorced while doing research for this book, co-parenting children was the topic that was most frequently brought up. I initially didn't plan on having a chapter on co-parenting, but such was the anxiety and concern of parents that I knew that this aspect of the divorce experience had to be addressed. I will outline three scenarios that will encompass a range of emotions that you will identify with as you try to be a great parent.

Before I share these three narratives, I need to emphasize the difficulty of co-parenting and being an effective sole parent whilst navigating your own personal journey of brokenness, as it calls for an amazing balancing act. Yet it is a function that will demand your total attention, as your child isn't divorced from your ex; only you are. Hence, despite the issues in your relationship with your ex, your children will still require you to be the best parent you can be. Though they will not relay to you the totality of their pain at seeing their parents in conflict, they will need even more reassurance from you than they usually would, as the separation brings with it a fair amount of collateral damage. as their parent, it is your responsibility to be acutely aware of their every need. It is easy to say, but I must warn you, it is incredibly difficult to get right all the time.

Six years after my divorce, my daughter told me she had won an award at her university and that there was going to be an exhibition of her work. Me, now the attentive parent, congratulated her on her achievements and looked forward to visiting the exhibition. After a few weeks, I asked my daughter when the exhibition would be, as nothing had been mentioned, and to my surprise, she said that the event was over and that I didn't need to worry about it as she had taken her mother to the exhibition. Of course, I replied that I had wanted to support her and see her exhibit. But then she said something that knocked me off my feet. "I didn't ask you to come because in the past you were always busy. Whether it was sports or work commitments, you never had the time. So what has changed now?" As I said, I was stunned, but I was also hurt. My quest to be there for her was genuine, but as she spoke, a newsreel of missed school plays and justified absences came rushing back at me. She was right; I had not been there in the past, so what was the big deal now?

One of the things we fail to comprehend is that our children grow up. And as adults, they don't just remember it all but live out the consequences of our actions and decisions as parents. These formative years are so crucial to their well-being. Of course, I'm not talking about perfection, I'm just saying that we have to be fully present and be there for our children, as they are, and always will be our primary concern.

Regardless of the reality of your divorce and the rationale behind the separation, every child wants Mummy and Daddy to be together. It gives them a warm, fuzzy feeling of safety and security. And research tells us that, despite our best efforts to shield our children from the emotional trauma, the effects of it, to them, will be timeless.

Ten years after the divorce, I was trying to arrange a birthday party for my daughter. As I was going through the details, it seemed that the frustrations of having two of everything had finally taken their toll: she had what I can only describe as a meltdown. We had never discussed the divorce in depth, as I had thought that the details should be between just her mother and me. But my daughter's suppressed emotions exploded as she relayed how torn the situation had made her feel and how upset she had been that no one asked her opinion or gave her a choice about whether the family should be broken up. She told me how, though I had pretended that all was well, my behavior would change if I saw her mother when I picked her up. She told stories of how, when I thought I was looking after her, she was in fact was looking after me. And then, as I grasped the full extent of her feelings, she spoke about the shock and the numbness she felt, which had now overflowed after years of silence.

She was right. As much as anyone tells you to get over it, there are so many reminders, anniversaries, birthdays, significant moments that matter and that take you back. And some anniversaries hold deeper scars, and those would take me on a cycle of wallowing and playing the victim that, as I said, sabotaged my healing and caused the 'paralysis.' It was within this self-destruct mode that I decided I had to take control. But it would seem that part of taking control was being upfront and honest with your children, acknowledging that, as much as you try to shield them from the emotions of the parental separation, children can always feel the temperature in the room, and they think they need to do something about it.

Being transparent allows them to be who they are rather than just reacting to whichever parent they need to make happy. The subliminal emotional demands placed on our children are not healthy and are not fair, as they are trying to heal too. Your love for your children needs to be unconditional and not connected to the right or wrong decisions they make within the divorce. Manipulating your ex by changing or withholding child visitations is unfair and damaging, as the child is as much part of your ex as they are part of you. Your children need you to be a strong parent, someone they can depend on and trust to be there for them, not someone who plays emotional games. They have already unwittingly blamed themselves for the breakdown of the relationship, and a culture of blame and conflict within the parental cycle will only add to the child's notion that the turmoil is their responsibility. It is imperative that you teach your children that there is a bright future after adjustment to the divorce. Children deserve to live a life of excitement and hope, knowing that healing, recovery and brighter days can be theirs, even if there is no marital reconciliation.

One of my clients, Bill, cried his heart out for many weeks when he saw the effect divorce was having on one of his children. He thought that if he was stoic and silent, the children would simply move on as he seemed to have moved on. Bill never spoke to his children about the separation from their mother. It was too painful for him, and he assumed it was too painful for them too. I remember him telling me one day how he was weeping inside as one of his daughters told him of her relationship issues, and at the end of her revelation, blamed her lack of relationship skills on never seeing her parents deal with conflict and differences in a constructive and healthy way. Because of that, she did what her parents did and said nothing in her relationship, hoping it would resolve itself. But alas, it did not. And now she was in a break-up scenario that was breaking her heart. As we all know, it is difficult to witness our children being in pain, and this is compounded by the hopelessness we feel ourselves which that accompanies the way we have dealt with issues in the past. Now we are witnesses to the consequences of our own behavior.

As we touched on earlier, providing a model of healthy behavior for our children whilst being in our own deep individual pain is torturous but necessary. The responsibility of navigating your children through the ever-changing environments that divorce brings will always be in the laps of the parents.

Communicating with my ex immediately after our separation was very strained and stressful. At times your parental rights seem to diminish, as the parent that your child lives with for the majority of the time seems to have become the primary decision-maker and now dictates the options, when before the parenting input was equal. This alteration within the parental equation finds you using phrases like, "Fighting for my rights" and "They're my children too." And yes, in essence, you're right, but this conflict will have an adverse effect on your children. You need to shield them from this type of dialogue and show them that Mummy and Daddy can still effectively parent despite the breakdown of the marriage. Here I would suggest that in the initial phases of the separation you communicate through a trusted third-party, for example grandparents, or correspond through text and email. This helps to minimize the flashpoints and conversely lessens the anxiety your children feel as they go from one parental situation to another. It is imperative that you don't deride or be disrespectful in any way to your ex in front of the children. Always esteem the other parent. You want your child to be respectful. And this will encourage and nurture a more inclusive atmosphere for your children. This will work for you in the long run, as the child will see your efforts to be balanced, fair and just.

I'm spending a lot of time on the idea of modelling healthy emotional interactions with your ex because the research tells us this has a serious and direct effect on the emotional well-being of your child. For instance, many children with divorced parents develop low self-esteem because they believe that they caused the divorce and then struggle with feelings of failure because they cannot keep Mummy and Daddy together. Your child may also display feelings of abandonment, especially when the parents remarry, as now the family they once knew no longer exists.

Dr Bob Barnes from 'Parenting on Purpose' advises that parents should focus on four key factors and in so doing cover the areas that are critical to the healing and growth of their child. He calls them the '4 Es'.

1. **Example**: We have discussed this at length already in this chapter.

2. **Encouragement**: At every opportunity, tell your child that you are proud of them. Words of affirmation from you will go a long way towards stabilizing their anxiety and will also allow your child to feel good about themselves. Your unconditional love and support will have an empowering effect as your child encounters the obstacles and challenges of life.

3. **Exposure**: Transparency with your child is another factor that is fundamental to their healing. It is crucial that they feel that they can come to you and discuss gender issues, issues of sexuality or being bullied. Being approachable about things that are often seen as taboo between parent and child helps to create and solidify a platform of safety and trust. Your openness and candor are key contributors to your child's healing.

4. Experience: I used to ask my young daughter, "Where do you want to eat?" if we were going out, and wherever she chose, we would go. At times, I wanted to go to other restaurants, but if I had asked her, I would honour that choice. I was letting her know that her decisions counted. I wanted her to be responsible for the choices she made, and this could only happen if I respected her choices.

The good news is that your children can heal from the experience of divorce. Your intentional quest to take the necessary steps towards an emotionally healthy future means that you will be rewarded by better days for yourself and your children. Those days are just ahead of you.

CO-PARENTING STRATEGY:

1. Be present and attentive to your children.
2. Model positive conflict resolution.
3. Establish a culture of love and create a safe space.
4. Use text and email as the main source of communication with your ex-partner.
5. Be your children's greatest fan—they need your affirmation.

STEP 7

WALKING INTO YOUR HEALING

"The wound is the place where the Light enters you."-Rumi

I wish you could see me now because I'm dancing, I really am. And whether you have moves like John Travolta or two left feet, you should be dancing too. Because to talk about or to be at the stage where you can talk about healing, shows just how incredibly resilient you are and and how determined you are to live a rich and flourishing life. The fact that you didn't let the pain, the anger, the helplessness, the loneliness, the humiliation and the overall sense of being out-of-control beat you is a testament to how amazing you are. And I will let you into a little secret—no, a big secret—that really helped me and transformed my thinking. "You didn't lose your partner, they lost an amazing you. And it's their loss, not yours." This will resonate with you more day-by-day as you walk through your journey with a healing heart, with a confidence, a bounce-in-your-step, such as you have never imagined. This new-found joy will open up new and exciting opportunities, and yes, you will become more attractive, not just to others, but more importantly, to yourself. When I started this journey of healing, I would often ask my support network, "What does healing look like?", as initially I needed a glimpse of my destination so that I would know where I was heading. And today my experience allows me to oblige you with an answer. Healing looks like loving yourself, being proud of yourself, focusing on improving yourself, being generous to others, being a giver, being grateful to others and building people up. It looks like appreciating others and life more by being a person that loves family, life and friends. Love and generosity don't stop when they are received by you, because life will present you with numerous opportunities to pass love on. Do this, and your life will be rewarding. The pain of infidelity causes us to contract, restrict or even block love, as love for us has turned into something toxic. But the new all-embracing you will not allow the obstacles of the past to curtail the beauty that lies ahead. Your healing and attitude of generosity will now compensate you richly. This reminds me of a quote I learned as a child,

"Give, and it will come back to you. A good measure, pressed down, shaken together and running over, will be poured into your lap."

I think that it is important to mention here that healing will never be final. It means always progressing towards wholeness but never quite getting there. And that's okay. As you journey forward, working with others toward ever-improving communication, your healing is being forged. Your healing will grow and mature you for a better today and an exciting tomorrow. Yet, healing works at different speeds for everyone, and there is no one-size-fits-all strategy for healing. Your journey is yours and will be very unique and individual to your emotions and circumstances. For me, it took years to recover, such was the depth of my pain, hurt and bitterness. It took a toll on my health, as un-forgiveness has physical consequences. It sets in motion such a chain of negativities that before I knew it, I was in a deep pit of denial, self-harm and isolation. I watched other people in similar distress healing faster than I, and I envied them, as they were emotionally further ahead of me. I learned to my detriment, but then to my benefit, that my journey is mine alone, that comparisons to others are not a healthy way to deal with these issues. I learned that I needed to listen to and focus on myself, that this attention to detail, to how I was advancing through the pitfalls and the successes, is central and fundamental to my ever-improving well-being.

In my research, I discovered that there is a school of thought that suggests that you are healed when you start dating again. I can understand why dating could be a barometer for wholeness and healing, as new sustainable relationships can be a great indicator of how far you have come. However, the issue here is that relationships are not just about your needs and wants but another person's too. It is essential that you understand that you need to be careful as you venture into new romantic relationships, as “Hurt people hurt people.”

You may not intend to hurt the other person, but I discovered something that nobody told me, as, unfortunately, I did hurt a few people along the way.

“When you open your heart, you open your wounds.”

Yes, my intentions were honourable, but after going through infidelity, you often ask yourself, “How can I also, during your healing, about you. And as you go through this process, you will scold yourself for being so blind to the now-obvious. “How did I not see this?” you will often wonder. Hence, it is imperative that this platform of doubt is destroyed and new pillars of trust are built. That is what we have been doing over these few chapters: rediscovering and building a better you.

So before you start dating, be aware that it is about you trusting yourself again: your sensors, your radar and your instincts. Remember that the process of healing has heightened your level of self-awareness like never before, and that is a good thing. Have a vision, a goal, a dream, and vow to be authentic through it all. You are now sensitive to the fact that there is no going back, that relationships change form, and that in those changes you are significant and worthy of good things happening to you. Surround yourself with people that lift you up, not people that take you down. Revive, renew and refresh yourself with books and literature that make you want to be a better you but also help you rediscover your old mojo. I found that reading helped, as at times, it is difficult to dampen the negative voices that take you down. Hence, I decided that the best course of action was to simply focus on amplifying the positives. This will enable you to drown out the doubts, questions, instability and fear that can at times torment us.

I don't want you to think that I'm against dating, but I do want to emphasise that the most important and primary relationship is the one you have with yourself. It is within this vortex of change that you will discover the awesomeness of you. Infidelity and all its issues have presented you with the opportunity to take stock and reflect, where at times we blissfully rush through life, not noticing or paying attention to the small, yet, significant details and signs. On your journey, I know for certain that as you recollect and ponder, you will see that it isn't always the major issues that have caused indifference, but a range of little things that didn't matter then but came to be of concern later. As I mentioned before, my first marriage workshop as a divorcee was entitled, "I wish I had paid attention." My experience has refocused me to the realisation that your needs and your healing require your total and focused attention.

But let's talk about dating, because I know that at the beginning of this book, dating seemed almost impossible to you, something that was very much in the distance, but here you are. Let me first say that we date in different ways, so these are not rules but principles to guide you through this next chapter of your healing.

Dating is fun and exciting; if you feel that you are not ready or you start to date but need time to recollect yourself and go at it again, do that. Remember to trust your instincts. You are a good person, an attractive person, who has grown in confidence, so just be you. Remember that you are a catch, and there is no need to settle, as the new improved you deserves to be in a relationship with someone who is as interested in your needs as you are in theirs.

Don't share your tale of infidelity from the outset, as it is unattractive. Also, please don't reveal all your flaws in one go. I did this once, as I had this newfound transparency-in-relationships idea to share. I think the first few new people I dated became Olympic sprinters, such was the unattractiveness of my story, and hence, me. Simply take a breath, take your time, and enjoy the moment. Remember that you are planting seeds, and the fruits will soon emerge. Enjoy being attentive and interested in someone else. Enjoy the exploration of someone else's views and experiences. As you take these steps, you will surprise yourself, because you have emerged into being a different person than the person who last dated. You will find that you have a deeper appreciation of the process. You will also feel more connected and significant as you seek to connect and make others feel significant. Remember in all of this that you are a giver and that you now trust that you are assured of your generosity being reciprocated. This mind-set will help you to give unashamedly, knowing that you have created a rich and rewarding cycle of fulfilled living for yourself.

For most of my life, I've suffered from insomnia, and because of that, I'm very thankful for American sports and recently the Internet, as they have kept me occupied. But in recent times, it has kept me very connected to people's pain, as, in my capacity as a Pastor and councillor, the majority of my work is about listening and being available to help people in their brokenness, which takes on many shapes. I remember there being a time when six women contacted me to talk about their trauma after being raped. Admittedly, I didn't have all the answers, but I listened with compassion and was able to connect them all with organisations and people who were better placed to serve their needs. Parallel to this, a stream of people who were going through divorce sought me out. I didn't personally know them, but all required some compassion and direction, as they felt lost and helpless. It reminded me of how, when you buy a new car, you begin to notice other people who are driving the same car as you.

I'm telling you this because I discovered something quite profound that will accelerate your healing. As I was helping others, I was being healed. I know it might sound crazy at first in this 21st-century world of "Where can you find the time?", but the secret to your wellness and growth will be found in you helping others. And in doing this, paradoxically, your pain will lessen as the encouragement and assistance you give to others brings you ever-closer to being whole again. There are many models of this method of healing, for example, that of 'Alcoholics Anonymous', where the unique relationship of accountability and compassion is linked to a journey of deep significance and healing. In playing your part in another's success, you are contributing to your own.

What a great note to end this book on. As you reflect on what you have read, I ask that you actively participate in your healing. Take action. Take the necessary steps.

Please don't return to the cycle of isolation. I did, and it is not healthy. Reach out. Get a counsellor, get a divorce coach. Surround yourself with people that will elevate you and encourage you on this journey. It doesn't have to be a large circle, but this is your fan club, and you are the CEO.

Thank you for taking the time to read this book. I am always available to you.

Every blessing and success in your healing.

Printed in Poland
by Amazon Fulfillment
Poland Sp. z o.o., Wrocław

54384400R00040